Scales for Jazz Improvisation

by Dan Haerle

A practice
method for all
instruments

MW01260026

STUDIO pr. publications recordings

ISBN 0-89898-705-9

9 780898 987058

Dan Haerle holds a Bachelor of Music degree from Coe College, Cedar Rapids, Iowa and a Master of Music degree from North Texas State University, Denton, Texas. For three years, he was a part-time instructor in the Jazz Department at North Texas State teaching arranging, improvisation, and directing various jazz groups. From North Texas State, he moved to Monterey Peninsula College, Monterey, California and was in charge of the jazz program directing the jazz ensemble, teaching improvisation and arranging, teaching jazz appreciation, and directing jazz piano workshops. From Sept. 1971 to June 1973, Mr. Haerle was the Assistant Professor of Music at the University of Miami, Coral Gables, Florida, assisting Mr. Jerry Coker in the instruction of arranging, jazz history, improvisation, jazz piano, and directing various jazz ensembles. He was a staff member of the Stan Kenton Jazz Clinic at the University of Redlands, Redlands, California for four years; a staff member of the Stan Kenton Jazz Clinic at Drury College in Springfield, Missouri for four years; a staff member of the Famous Arrangers' Clinic, University of Nevada, Las Vegas, Nevada for three years; and a staff member of the National Stage Band Camps for three years. Mr. Haerle has had extensive performing experience as a studio organist and pianist, as a pianist with the Faculty Jazz Quartet at the University of Miami, and as a summer replacement for Stan Kenton with the Stan Kenton Orchestra.

TABLE OF CONTENTS

INTRODUCTION

The purpose of this syllabus is to present, in as concise a form as possible, the scales which are used in improvisation. The book, which shows the scales in treble and bass clef in all keys, is intended as a practice manual. The syllabus should be considered an aid to eventually memorizing the scales in all keys. A thorough understanding of the interval structure of each scale form, as it is practiced, will greatly speed up this process.

In addition to the scales themselves, explanations are included as to the application of each scale form to one or more chord types. Also, charts showing the relationship of certain scales to each other are included. Finally, some suggestions are made as to how to practice the scales to learn them thoroughly.

GENERAL NOTES

1. Unless otherwise indicated, all scales in this book are constructed on the root of the chord to which they relate.

2. The words mode and scale mean the same thing.

3. In the *Guide To Scale Choice* chart, the chord type is dictated either by a given chord progression or by personal taste.

4. In a II-V-I progression in a major key, the Dorian, Mixolydian, and Major scales which accompany those chords all have the same key signature.

5. In a II-V-I progression in a minor key, the Harmonic Minor scale of the key may be used with all three chords.

6. An * beside the name of a scale indicates that it has no "wrong" notes, or notes which would sound intolerably dissonant if emphasized.

7. The scales in the syllabus are not arranged in order of difficulty or importance but, instead, are grouped in what seem to be logical categories.

8. Those modes of the Melodic and Harmonic Minor scales which are rarely used have not been presented in all keys. It is felt that the serious student, interested in pursuing the creative possibilities of those scales, will be able to supply the necessary transpositions.

9. If it is indicated that a scale is used with a certain family of chords, it will work with any size chord in that family (triad, 7th, 9th, 11th or 13th).

4

SUGGESTIONS FOR PRACTICE

1. Scales should be practiced <u>with a metronome</u>, <u>in all keys</u>, at different rhythmic levels such as the following examples.

When practicing, stress absolute rhythmic evenness and flawless execution. Concentrate on tone, pitch and articulation as well.

2. Scales should be practiced over the entire range of the instrument, from the lowest note of the scale found on the instrument to the highest.

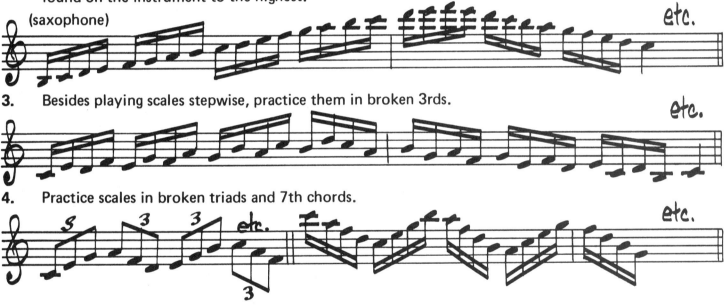

3. Besides playing scales stepwise, practice them in broken 3rds.

4. Practice scales in broken triads and 7th chords.

5. Finally, play all over the scale, over the full range of your instrument, using stepwise motion and leaps of larger intervals.

6. Strive for speed and ease in playing scales. This will help both in developing facility and in thoroughly learning the scale. Begin by practicing a scale only as fast as you can play it perfectly and gradually increase your speed from that point. Marking metronome markings on the scale page to remind you of your most recent stage of progress will help avoid wasting time.

SECTION I

MODES GENERATED BY THE MAJOR SCALE

Chart is based on C Major scale:

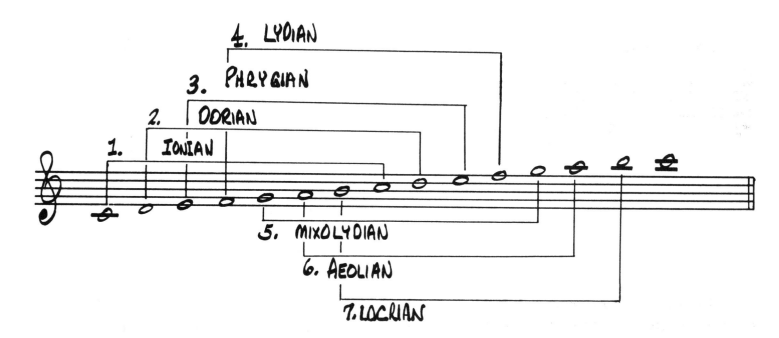

1.   C to C generates the C Ionian (Major) scale.

2.   D to D generates the D Dorian scale.

3.   E to E generates the E Phrygian scale.

4.   F to F generates the F Lydian scale.

5.   G to G generates the G Mixolydian scale.

6.   A to A generates the A Aeolian (pure minor) scale.

7.   B to B generates the B Locrian scale.

THE IONIAN (MAJOR) SCALE

The Ionian scale is known to most people simply as the major scale. It is constructed of 5 whole steps and 2 half steps. The half steps occur between steps 3 and 4 and steps 7 and 8 of the scale.

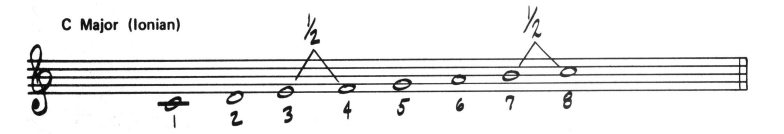

The Ionian (major) scale is used with major family chords such as the major triad, major 7th and major 6-9 chord. The scale cannot be used when a chromatic alteration foreign to the scale is present in the harmony (example #5 or #11). There are other scale forms especially suited for those occasions.

In using the scale, it is important to remember that the 4th scale step is dissonant to a major chord. It has a strong tendency to resolve to the 3rd of the chord. Also, if the major 7th is present in the chord, the 1st (8th) scale step is relatively dissonant. It has a tendency to "resolve" to the 7th.

Because of the potential dissonance of the 1st and 4th scale steps, the "pretty" notes of the scale are the other five scale steps (2, 3, 5, 6, and 7). It will be found that these scales steps form a minor pentatonic scale which could be constructed on the 3rd of a major chord. This application will be examined more closely in the section on pentatonic scales.

IONIAN (MAJOR) SCALES

THE DORIAN SCALE *

The Dorian scale is constructed of 5 whole steps and 2 half steps. The half steps occur between steps 2 and 3 and steps 6 and 7 of the scale.

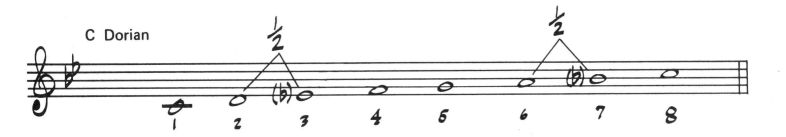

There are three ways of conceiving a Dorian scale:

1) A pure minor scale with a raised 6th scale step.

2) A major scale with lowered 3rd and 7th scale steps.

3) A scale bearing the same key signature as the major scale located a whole step below (C Dorian has the key signature of B-flat major).

The Dorian scale is used with minor family chords which do not include any alterations. It will be found that the Dorian scale is comprised of all of the tones of a complete minor 13th chord. Therefore, there are no "wrong" notes in the sense of a "clinker" that is terribly dissonant to the harmony. Any tone in the scale will sound acceptable with an unaltered minor harmony. However, the choice of one note over another may be unfortunate in a musical sense, naturally.

The Dorian scale is generally used with minor chords which function as a I, II or IV chord in a major or minor key. If the minor chord occurs as a III or VI chord, the Phrygian or Aeolian scale may be a better choice.

DORIAN SCALES *

THE PHRYGIAN SCALE

The Phrygian scale is constructed of 5 whole steps and 2 half steps. The half steps occur between steps 1 and 2 and steps 5 and 6 of the scale.

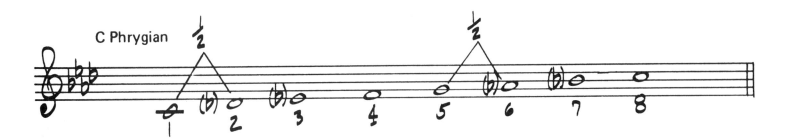

There are three ways of conceiving a Phrygian scale:

1) A pure minor scale with a lowered 2nd scale step.

2) A major scale with lowered 2nd, 3rd, 6th, and 7th scale steps.

3) A scale bearing the same key signature as the major scale located a major 3rd below (C Phrygian has the same key signature as A-flat major).

The Phrygian scale is probably most used in playing compositions which are written in the Phrygian mode. Such pieces often have a strong tonal center which is either of a long duration or returns often throughout the progression. The 2nd and 6th scale steps are dissonant and want to resolve downward to the 1st and 5th steps of the scale.

The Phrygian scale is also used with minor chords which function as III or VI chords in a major key though the Aeolian scale may be a better choice for the VI chord.

PHRYGIAN SCALES

THE LYDIAN SCALE *

The Lydian scale is constructed of 5 whole steps and 2 half steps. The half steps occur between steps 4 and 5 and steps 7 and 8 of the scale.

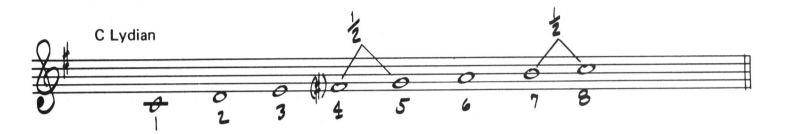

There are two ways of conceiving a Lydian scale:

1) A major scale with a raised 4th scale step.

2) A scale bearing the same key signature as the major scale located a perfect 4th below (C Lydian has the same key signature as G Major).

The Lydian scale is used with major family chords especially when the ♯11 occurs in the harmony. When a ♭5 occurs in the chord, the Lydian scale is also a good choice. However, alteration of the major chord is not necessary for the use of this scale. The ♯4 in the scale eliminates the problem of the dissonant 4th of the major scale and may be emphasized without resolution.

Like the major scale, the 1st scale step may be fairly dissonant when the major 7th is present in the harmony. It has the same tendency to resolve down to the 7th.

All of the tones of the scale besides the 1st (or 8th) are "pretty" notes to use with major harmonies. It will be found that there are two minor pentatonic scales within these six tones of the scale. One can be built on the 3rd of the chord (using steps 3, 5, 6, 7, and 2) and the other can be built on the 7th (using steps 7, 2, 3, ♯4, and 6). This will be elaborated on in the section on pentatonic scales.

THE MIXOLYDIAN (DOMINANT) SCALE

The Mixolydian scale is constructed of 5 whole steps and 2 half steps. The half steps occur between steps 3 and 4 and steps 6 and 7 of the scale.

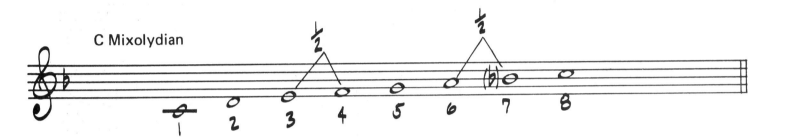

There are two ways of conceiving a Mixolydian scale:

1) A major scale with a lowered 7th scale step.

2) A scale bearing the same key signature as the major scale located a perfect 4th above (C Mixolydian has the same key signature as F major).

The Mixolydian mode (sometimes called the dominant scale) is used with dominant family harmonies which have no alterations present such as ♭5 or ♯5, ♭9 or ♯9, or ♯11. The 4th scale step is very dissonant to a dominant 7th chord and has a strong tendency to resolve downward to the 3rd of the chord. This resolution creates a motive which has been the originating germ for many "bluesy" ideas. Any other tone of the scale may be emphasized without fear of it sounding wrong.

The Mixolydian scale is also used when there is a suspended 4th present in a dominant 7th chord. In this case, the 4th should receive the emphasis rather than the 3rd of the chord.

MIXOLYDIAN (DOMINANT) SCALES

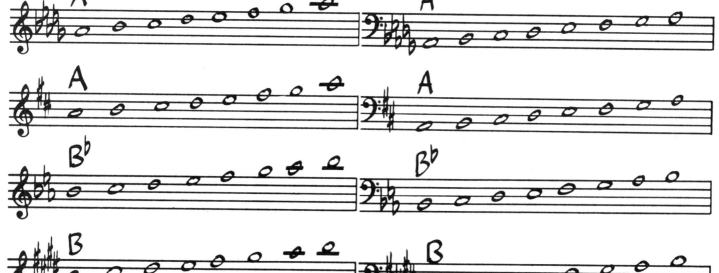

THE AEOLIAN (PURE MINOR) SCALE

The Aeolian scale is constructed of 5 whole steps and 2 half steps. The half steps occur between steps 2 and 3 and steps 5 and 6 of the scale.

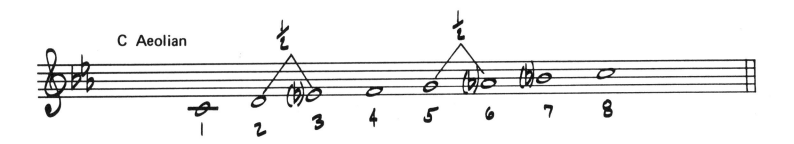

There are three ways of conceiving an Aeolian scale:

1) A pure minor scale.

2) A major scale with lowered 3rd, 6th and 7th scale steps.

3) A scale bearing the same key signature as the major scale located 3 half steps above (its relative major).

The Aeolian scale is used with minor family chords which do not include any alterations. The 6th scale step is dissonant to a minor chord and has the tendency to resolve downward to the 5th of the chord.

The Aeolian mode is generally best used on minor chords which function as either a III or VI chord in a major key. When the minor chord assumes the function of a I or II chord, the Dorian scale is generally a better choice.

AEOLIAN (PURE MINOR) SCALES

THE LOCRIAN SCALE

The Locrian scale is constructed of 5 whole steps and 2 half steps. The half steps occur between steps 1 and 2 and steps 4 and 5 of the scale.

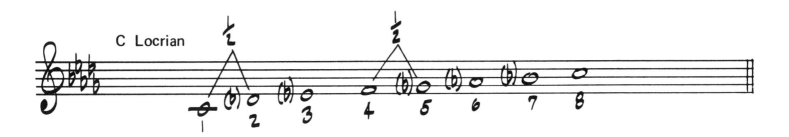

There are three ways of conceiving a Locrian scale:

1) A pure minor scale with lowered 2nd and 5th scale steps.

2) A major scale with lowered 2nd, 3rd, 5th, 6th and 7th scale steps.

3) A scale bearing the same key signature as the major scale located a half step above (C Locrian has the same key signature as D-flat major).

The Locrian mode is often called the half-diminished scale. It is used with a minor 7th chord with a lowered 5th (also called a half-diminished chord). The 2nd scale step is dissonant to a half-diminished chord and has a tendency to resolve downward to the root of the chord.

If the Locrian scale is used with a half-diminished chord which has the unaltered 9th present, the 2nd scale step must be raised to avoid a dissonant clash with the harmony.

LOCRIAN SCALES

SECTION II

MODES GENERATED BY THE

ASCENDING MELODIC MINOR SCALE

Chart is based on C melodic minor scale:

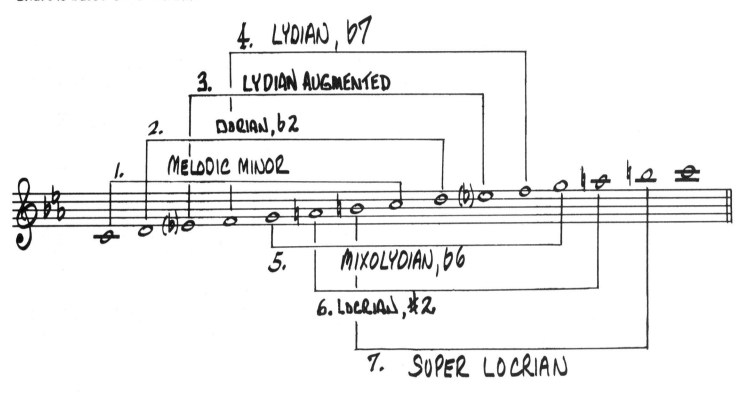

1. C to C generates the C melodic minor scale.

2. D to D generates the D Dorian, ♭2 scale (uncommon, not included).

3. E♭ to E♭ generates the E♭ Lydian Augmented scale.

4. F to F generates the F Lydian, ♭7 scale.

5. G to G generates the Mixolydian, ♭6 scale (uncommon, not included).

6. A to A generates the Locrian, ♯2 scale.

7. B to B generates the Super Locrian scale.

The Ascending Melodic Minor scale is constructed of 5 whole steps and 2 half steps. The half steps occur between steps 2 and 3 and steps 7 and 8 of the scale.

There are two ways of conceiving a Melodic Minor scale:

1) A pure minor scale with raised 6th and 7th scale steps.

2) A major scale with a lowered 3rd.

The Melodic Minor scale is used with a minor family chord which has a raised 7th. It may also be implied by playing the raised 7th scale step as a passing tone between the root and 7th of a conventional minor 7th chord. When the scale is used with a mi ♯7 chord, any scale tone may be emphasized without fear of an intolerable dissonance occurring. One exception is that the root of the chord may have a tendency to resolve downward to the raised 7th of the chord.

MELODIC MINOR SCALES *

23

THE LYDIAN-AUGMENTED SCALE *

The Lydian-Augmented scale is constructed of 5 whole steps and 2 half steps. The half steps occur between steps 5 and 6 and steps 7 and 8 of the scale.

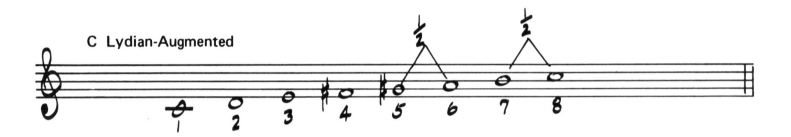

There are two ways of conceiving a Lydian-Augmented scale:

1) A major scale with raised 4th and 5th scale steps.

2) A scale which has the same tones as a melodic minor scale built on the note three half steps below. (C Lydian-Augmented is the same as A melodic minor)

The Lydian-Augmented scale is used with a major family chord which has a raised 5th. Though implied by the scale, the #11 need not be present in the harmony.

As in a major scale, the root of this scale may be dissonant to the major 7th of the chord. It has the same tendency to resolve downward to the 7th. All other tones in the scale may be emphasized without concern.

THE LYDIAN, ♭7 SCALE *

The Lydian, ♭7 scale is sometimes called the Lydian-Dominant scale. It is constructed of 5 whole steps and 2 half steps. The half steps occur between steps 4 and 5 and steps 6 and 7.

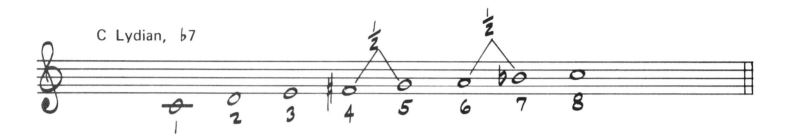

There are three ways of conceiving a Lydian, ♭7 scale:

1) A Lydian scale with a lowered 7th scale step.

2) A Mixolydian scale with a raised 4th scale step.

3) A scale which has the same tones as a melodic minor scale built on the note a perfect 4th below. (C Lydian, b7 is the same as G melodic minor)

The Lydian, ♭7 scale is used with dominant family chords which are unaltered with the exception of the ♯11 which may or may not be present. By raising the 4th of a Mixolydian mode to create this scale, the dissonance of the unaltered 4th disappears. Therefore, any tone in the scale may be emphasized without fear of it sounding like a "wrong" note.

When the ♯11 is present in a dominant chord, the Lydian, ♭7 is definitely a preferable choice over the Mixolydian scale. This is because the unaltered 4th of the Mixolydian mode would cause a dissonant clash with the ♯11.

A Lydian, ♭7 scale has the same tones as a Super Locrian scale built on the note located a tri-tone above or below. This information is useful in improvising on progressions which involve tri-tone substitutions of dominant chords.

LYDIAN, ♭7 SCALES *

THE LOCRIAN, ♯2 SCALE *

The Locrian, ♯2 scale is constructed of 5 whole steps and 2 half steps. The half steps occur between steps 2 and 3 and steps 4 and 5 of the scale.

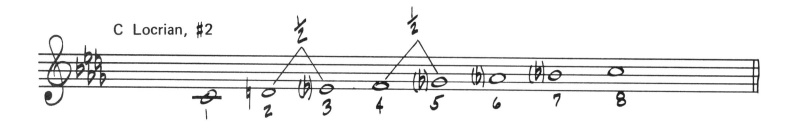

There are four ways of conceiving a Locrian, ♯2 scale:

1) A Locrian scale with a raised 2nd scale step.

2) A pure minor scale with a lowered 5th scale step.

3) A major scale with lowered 3rd, 5th, 6th and 7th scale steps.

4) A scale which has the same tones as a melodic minor scale built on the note three half steps above. (C Locrian, ♯2 is the same as Eb melodic minor)

The Locrian, ♯2 scale is used with a minor 7th chord which has a lowered 5th (half-diminished chord). Any tone in the scale may be emphasized without fear of it sounding "wrong". When the unaltered 9th is present in the harmony, this scale should be chosen in preference to the pure Locrian mode. This is because the lowered 2nd scale step in the Locrian mode would create a dissonant clash with the 9th of the chord.

LOCRIAN #2 SCALES *

29

THE SUPER LOCRIAN SCALE *

This scale has many names all of which are really correct and commonly used. It is called the Altered Dominant scale, the Pomeroy scale, the Ravel scale, and the Diminished-Whole Tone scale. However, the classical name is the Super Locrian scale.

It is constructed of 5 whole steps and 2 half steps. The half steps occur between steps 1 and 2 and steps 3 and 4 of the scale.

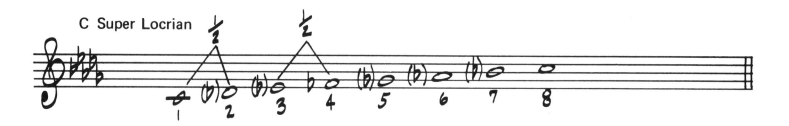

There are two ways of conceiving a Super Locrian scale:

1) A Locrian scale with a lowered 4th scale step.

2) A scale which has the same tones as a melodic minor scale built on the note a half step above. (C Super Locrian is the same as Db melodic minor)

The Super Locrian scale is used with dominant family chords which have both an altered 5th and an altered 9th present in any combination (-5-9, -5+9, +5-9, +5+9). The chord may include both altered 5ths and both altered 9ths since all of these alterations occur as scale tones in the Super Locrian scale.

If the dominant chord is lacking either an altered 5th or an altered 9th, the whole tone or diminished scale may be a better choice. This should be apparent due to the altered nature of the scale.

A Super Locrian scale has the same tones as a Lydian, ♭7 scale built on the note located a tri-tone above or below. This information is useful in improvising on progressions which involve tri-tone substitutions of dominant chords.

SUPER LOCRIAN SCALES *

31

SYMMETRICAL ALTERED SCALES

THE CHROMATIC SCALE

The Chromatic scale is constructed exclusively of half steps. Therefore, there is really only <u>one</u> Chromatic scale which may begin on any tone.

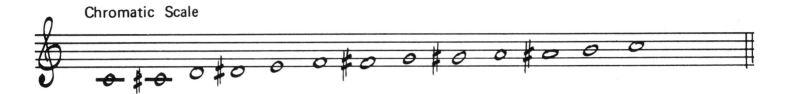

Chromatic Scale

The Chromatic scale may be used with <u>any</u> chord type with any combination of alterations. Naturally, some scale tones will always be dissonant to the harmony and have a strong tendency to resolve. This resolution will probably always be either up or down a half step to the nearest chord tone.

Chromatic motion can create excitement if used sparingly. If more than 4 or 5 successive chromatic scale steps are used, the musical style may become more "cocktailish" in character. This is because of the proliferation of "rippling" chromatic runs found in much commercial music. However, short chromatic "bursts" of notes can generate melodic energy and certainly should not be avoided.

THE WHOLE TONE SCALE *

The Whole Tone scale is constructed exclusively of whole steps, 6 in all. As there are only 12 tones in the chromatic scale, this means that there are only <u>two</u> different sounding whole tone scales. Each of those two scales can be interpreted enharmonically as several different scales.

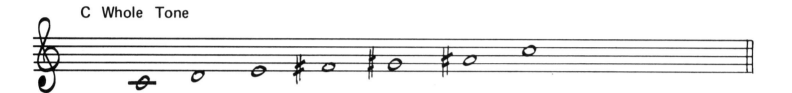

C Whole Tone

A whole tone scale, by its nature, omits one letter of the musical alphabet in its spelling. This creates the interval of a diminished 3rd between two of the scale tones. The diminished 3rd (which is the same as a whole step) may occur between any two notes of the scale. An understanding of this fact should help avoid confusion in constructing the scale.

The Whole Tone scale is used with dominant family chords which have either a raised or lowered 5th or both. It can be seen that both of these alterations are present in the scale. However, if a lowered 5th is present, a Lydian, ♭7 scale would be an acceptable choice instead of the Whole Tone scale.

If an altered 9th is present in the harmony, the Whole Tone scale cannot be used because of the dissonant clash with the unaltered 9th which is present in the scale.

Because of its symmetry, the Whole Tone scale is capable of generating many patterns which move up or down through the scale at some regular interval. Whole Tone patterns were commonly used by many players in the Bebop era.

WHOLE TONE SCALES *

THE WHOLE STEP-HALF STEP DIMINISHED SCALE *

The Diminished scale is constructed of 4 whole steps and 4 half steps in regular alternation. As a result, there are only <u>three</u> different sounding diminished scales. Each one of those scales can be interpreted enharmonically as several different scales.

Since the diminished scale has 8 tones, one letter of the musical alphabet (besides the root) will be repeated in the spelling of the scale. This should not cause any confusion because the repeated letter may occur anywhere in the scale.

The Whole Step-Half Step Diminished scale is used with the diminished 7th chord. Within the scale are found the 4 tones of a diminished 7th chord and 4 tones which are located a whole step above the tones of the chord. These are the notes that are commonly added to a dim7 chord to color it or fill it out. Therefore, any tone of the scale will sound acceptable with a dim7 chord and may be emphasized without concern.

This scale may also be used with a half-diminished chord which leads to a dominant chord a 5th below. Some notes clash slightly but the dissonance disappears as the chord changes.

Because of its symmetry, the Diminished scale is capable of generating many patterns which move up or down through the scale at some regular interval. Diminished patterns are commonly used today.

Of course, this scale is really the same as the half-whole diminished scale starting on a different note. The advantage of conceiving this scale as beginning with a whole step is that it may then be constructed on the root of the chord that it accompanies.

WHOLE STEP, HALF STEP DIMINISHED SCALES*

THE HALF STEP-WHOLE STEP DIMINISHED SCALE *

The Diminished scale is constructed of 4 half steps and 4 whole steps in regular alternation. As a result, there are only <u>three</u> different sounding diminished scales. Each one of those scales can be interpreted enharmonically as several different scales.

C Half Step-Whole Step Diminished

Since the diminished scale has 8 tones, one letter of the musical alphabet (besides the root) will be repeated in the spelling of the scale. This should not cause any confusion because the repeated letter may occur anywhere in the scale.

The Half Step-Whole Step Diminished scale is used with a dominant 7th family chord which has either a raised or lowered 9th or both present. It can be seen that both of these alterations are present in the scale. The other scale tones are the root, 3rd, 5th, ♭7th, ♯11th and 13th.

If a raised 5th is present in the harmony, the Diminished scale cannot be used because of the dissonant clash with the unaltered 5th present in the scale. If a lowered 5th is present in the chord, the diminished scale could be used but would be a less good choice than Super Locrian.

Because of its symmetry, the Diminished scale is capable of generating many patterns which move up or down through the scale at some regular interval. Diminished patterns are commonly used today.

Of course, this scale is really the same as the whole-half diminished scale starting on a different note. The advantage of conceiving this scale as beginning with a half step is that it may then be constructed on the root of the chord that it accompanies.

HALF STEP, WHOLE STEP DIMINISHED SCALES *

THE AUGMENTED SCALE

The Augmented scale is constructed of 3 half steps and 3 intervals of a minor 3rd (augmented 2nd). These minor 3rds occur in regular alternation with the half steps. As a result, there are only <u>four</u> different sounding Augmented scales. Each of those scales can be interpreted enharmonically as several different scales.

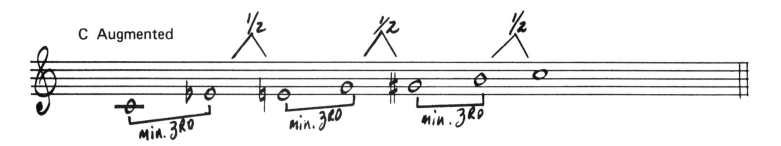

Since there are only 6 tones in the Augmented scale, one letter of the musical alphabet will be omitted in the spelling of this scale. This omission could occur at any point in the scale.

The Augmented scale is used with major family chords which have a raised 5th present in the harmony. There are actually six augmented triads, the roots of which form two augmented triads, in the scale. There are also three major triads present in the scale.

Because of its symmetry, the Augmented scale is capable of generating patterns which move up or down through the scale at some regular interval. These are less common than whole tone or diminished patterns but sound very effective.

AUGMENTED SCALES

40

SECTION IV

MISCELLANEOUS SCALES

Major Pentatonic Scale

Minor Pentatonic Scale

Blues Scale

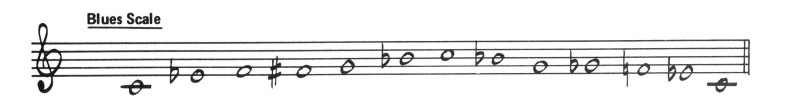

Harmonic Minor Scale

The Major Pentatonic scale is constructed of 3 whole steps and 2 intervals of a minor 3rd. The minor 3rds occur between steps 3 and 4 and steps 5 and 6.

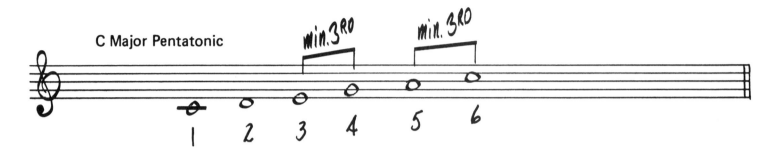

The Major Pentatonic scale is used with major family chords which have no alterations present. However, it may be constructed on notes other than the root of a chord to produce a number of harmonic sonorities. Examples are given below to show several uses of the same Major Pentatonic scale. The scale tones are analyzed in relation to each chord type.

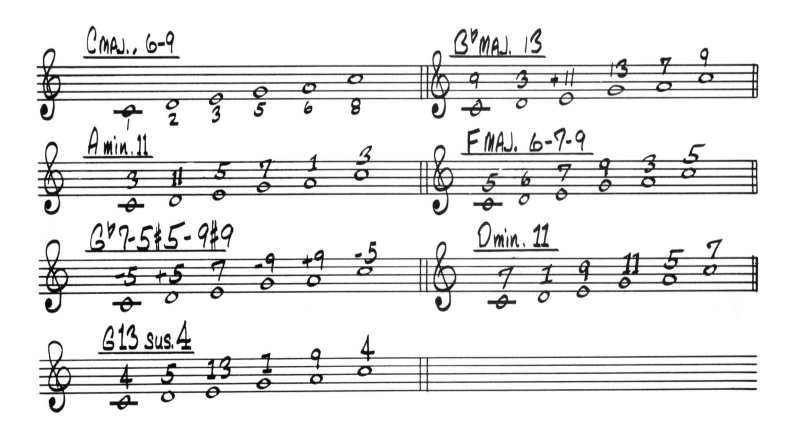

MAJOR PENTATONIC SCALES *

THE MINOR PENTATONIC SCALE *

The Minor Pentatonic scale is constructed of 3 whole steps and two intervals of a minor 3rd. The minor 3rds occur between steps 1 and 2 and steps 4 and 5 of the scale.

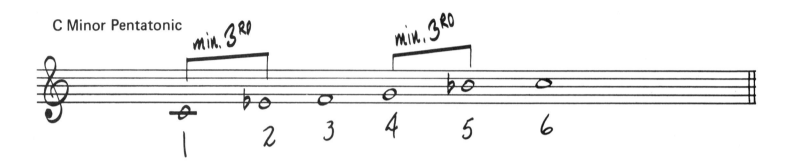

The Minor Pentatonic scale is used with minor family chords which have no alterations present. However, it may be constructed on notes other than the root of a chord to produce a number of harmonic sonorities. Examples are given below to show several uses of the same Minor Pentatonic scale. The scale tones are analyzed in relation to each chord type.